WG

The Wisdom
of the West

The Wisdom
of the West

Common Sense and Uncommon Genius
From 101 Great Westerners

Compiled and Edited by Criswell Freeman

WALNUT GROVE PRESS
Nashville, TN 37205

ISBN 1-887655-31-X

The ideas expressed in this book are not, in all cases, exact quotations, as some have been edited for clarity and brevity. In all cases, the author has attempted to maintain the speaker's original intent. In some cases, material for this book was obtained from secondary sources, primarily print media. While every effort was made to ensure the accuracy of these sources, the accuracy cannot be guaranteed. For additions, deletions, corrections or clarifications in future editions of this text, please write WALNUT GROVE PRESS.

Printed in the United States of America
Cover Design by Mary Mazer
Typesetting & Page Layout by Sue Gerdes
Editor for Walnut Grove Press: Alan Ross
1 2 3 4 5 6 7 8 9 10 • 97 98 99 00 01

ACKNOWLEDGMENTS
The author gratefully acknowledges the helpful support of Angela Beasley, Dick and Mary Freeman, and Mary Susan Freeman.

For Virginia and Patricia

The Fabulous Kelley Sisters

Table of Contents

Introduction

The Spanish explorer Juan Vásquez de Coronado described the West in this way: "The Country itself is the best I have ever seen for producing all the products of Spain. But what I am sure of is that there is not any gold or any other metal in all of that country." So much for bold predictions.

Had he lived long enough to watch the 49ers pry tons of gold from the California soil, Coronado would have learned an important lesson: Never underestimate the West.

From the Mississippi to the Pacific, America's western region is simply too big for exaggeration, too diverse for simplification, and too rich for depreciation.

The West has produced a fascinating mixture of pioneers, heroes, scoundrels and rogues. This book serves as a concise collection of their insights and humor.

The wisdom herein was acquired the hard way. In the days of tepees and sod huts, Westerners learned about courage. On the wagon trains, they learned about determination. The gold fields taught them about hope. As the Great West was gradually tamed, a unique brand of wisdom was stamped into the collective consciousness of its citizens.

Westerners treasure independence. They share a common love of nature and a common distrust of fences. Their dreams are big enough and bold enough to match the landscape. So consider carefully the insightful nuggets that follow because, Coronado notwithstanding, there's gold in them there pages.

1

The West

James Bryce, a 19th century British statesman, author and world traveler, made his first visit to the American West in 1870. He observed, "It is the same everywhere from the Pacific to the Mississippi. Men seem to live in the future rather than the present. They see the country not merely as it is, but as it will be twenty, fifty, one hundred years hence."

The West was won by a dizzying assortment of dreamers, visionaries, heroes and crackpots. But these men and women, despite their differences, shared one common trait: They were all futurists. The following quotations describe the world they discovered and the world they built.

Westward the course of the empire takes its way.

George Berkely, 1752

Eastward I go only by force, but Westward I go free. The future lies that way for me.

Henry David Thoreau

The natural tide of emigration
of the human race tends westward.

Cass G. Barns

The American claim is by right
of our manifest destiny to overspread and
to possess the whole of the continent
which Providence has given us.

John Louis O'Sullivan

Four centuries from the discovery of
America, at the end of a hundred years of life
under the Constitution, the frontier has gone
and with its going has closed the first period
of American history.

Frederick Jackson Turner

The achieved West had given
the United States something that
no people had ever had before,
an internal, domestic empire.

Bernard De Voto

The West may be called
the most distinctively
American part of America.

James Bryce

I think that the West is the most powerful reality in the history of America.

J. S. Holliday

West of the Mississippi
　　　it's a little more look, see, act;
　　a little less rationalize, comment, talk.
F. Scott Fitzgerald

Out where the handclasp's a little stronger,
　out where the smile dwells a little longer.
　　That's where the West begins.
Arthur Chapman

Waterways in the East;
　　wagonways in the West.
Pioneer Slogan

The history of the West is one of the great
stories of all time. But no intelligent person
　can look at it without feeling a mixture
　　　of both pride and shame.
T. H. Watkins

The West is color. Its colors are animal
rather than vegetable, the colors of
earth and sunlight and ripeness.

Jessamyn West

Crowds were drawn to the West for reasons
of personal adventure, or because the
romantic legends of the West attracted them.
People were drawn by the intangibles,
the touch of the wind on their faces,
a return to the simple elements of living.

Edith Ammons Kohl

The abundance of vacant land operates as
the safety valve of our system.

George Bancroft, 1832

When the railroad met the buffalo,
the Iron Age met the Stone Age, the machine
arrived in the garden, and the West
was changed forever.

T. H. Watkins

We seem on the threshold of a destiny
higher and better than any nation has yet
fulfilled. And the great West is to rule us.

Albert Deane Richardson

The West is hope's native home.

Wallace Stegner

I knew that a great destiny waited for me in the West.

Sam Houston

Go West, young man and grow up with the country.

Horace Greeley

2

All-Purpose Advice

The West was not settled by busybodies. In fact, an old frontier adage warned "Never give salt nor advice until it's asked for." With apologies to pioneers everywhere, the following words of wisdom are offered without prior solicitation.

We are all here for a spell;
    get all the good laughs you can.

Will Rogers

Make each day your masterpiece.

John Wooden

In the time of your life, live.

William Saroyan

You do not create a style.
You work and develop yourself; your style is
    an emanation from your own being.

Katherine Anne Porter

Always be in a state of becoming.

Walt Disney

Don't just grab the first thing that comes by.
Know what to turn down.

Will Rogers

Anytime anybody tells me the trend
is such and such, I do the opposite.

Clint Eastwood

It is best for thinking people to change
their minds occasionally in order to keep
them clean. For those who do not think,
it is best at least to rearrange
their prejudices once in a while.

Luther Burbank

Inaction may be the highest form of action.

Jerry Brown

Live so that you
wouldn't mind selling
your pet parrot
to the town gossip.

Will Rogers

The only things in the middle of the road are yellow stripes and dead armadillos.

Jim Hightower

My business philosophy?
Don't be in too big a hurry, don't get excited,
and don't lose your sense of humor. You can't
be objective and emotional at the same time.

Sid Richardson

The best public relations are based
on good deeds.

Stanley Marcus

The world doesn't care why you can't get
the job done. It only pays off on results.

Bum Bright

Get a good idea and stay with it,
and work it until it's done and done right.

Walt Disney

Think twice before you speak
         to a friend in need.

Ambrose Bierce

The time to save is now.
  When a dog gets a bone, he doesn't go out
and make a down payment on a bigger bone.
      He buries the one he's got.

Will Rogers

God enriches.

Arizona State Motto

I've always followed my father's advice.
He told me, first, to always keep my word;
second, to never insult anybody intentionally;
and, third, not to go around
looking for trouble.

John Wayne

Talk low, talk slow, and don't say too much.

John Wayne

No one has a finer command of the language
than the person who keeps his mouth shut.

Sam Rayburn

Do the best you can, and don't take life too serious.

Will Rogers

3

Courage

In the 17th century, the French moralist Francois De La Rochefoucauld observed, "The only security is courage." These words were particularly true on the Western frontier.

The Old West was no place for sissies. Opportunity was everywhere, but so was danger. Settlers were forced to act accordingly.

"Keep your courage up," one pioneer advised, "and it will keep you up." And what should a man do if, heaven forbid, he lost his nerve? Move back East, of course.

The Western man of the
old days had little choice
but to be courageous.

Walter Prescott Webb

Courage can achieve everything.

Sam Houston

Courage

What most Western women had
in their faces was character. Survival was
more important than prettiness.

Alice Marriott

Let them come on foot with handcarts
or wheelbarrows; let them gird up their loins
and walk through, and nothing shall hinder
or stay them.

Brigham Young

The cowards never started.

The Society of California

There's right and there's wrong.
You get to do one or the other. You do one,
and you're living. You do the other,
and you may be walking around,
but you're as dead as a beaver hat.

John Wayne

You have to have faith in yourself.
If you have no goal, if you don't know where
you're headed, you will never reach
the port of success.

Simon Benson

Defeat in this world is no disgrace if you
fought well and fought for the right thing.

Katherine Anne Porter

There is a giant asleep in every man.
When that giant awakes, miracles happen.

Frederick Faust

Courage

We have food enough for one meal
and rely with confidence on the inscrutable
ways of Providence to send in our road
wherewith to subsist on from day to day.

Robert Stuart, 1812

The young man who has the nerve
to leave the drudgery of the mill and factory
and strike out for himself will succeed
in the West.

Murdo Coyote, 1907

One of the marks of a gift is to have
the courage to pursue it.

Katherine Anne Porter

The quintessential American heroes
are Westerners.

Richard White

Courage is always safer than cowardice.

Frontier Saying

Courage is the price life
exacts for granting peace.

Amelia Earhart

4

Hard Work

Theodore Roosevelt was a privileged New Yorker who learned about hard work in the wilderness of the West. He said, "I wish to preach, not the doctrine of ignoble ease, but the doctrine of the strenuous life." In his search for insight into the "strenuous life," Teddy could not have picked a better training ground than the Old West.

In Roosevelt's day, every man was responsible for earning his own chow. On the frontier, there were no paid holidays and no social safety nets, so work was not optional for the man who had grown accustomed to food. The following quotations provide a glimpse into the work ethic of the West. Teddy Roosevelt would have been proud.

Far and away the best prize life offers is the chance to work hard at work worth doing.

Theodore Roosevelt

What the country needs
is dirtier fingernails
and cleaner minds.

Will Rogers

One flies with one's own wings.
Oregon Pioneer Association Poster, 1876

Rich rewards come to the strong
and the steadfast.
Yankton Press and Dakotan

Don't sit down and wait for the cow
to back up to be milked. Get up
and go after the cow.
Kadoka Press

Here there is abundant room for all good
citizens, and no room for loafers or bummers.
Benjamin Singleton

Produce what you consume.

Brigham Young's Dictum

The West. In the hands of an enterprising
people, what a country this might be.
Richard Henry Dana

Luck is what happens when preparation
meets opportunity.
Darrell Royal

When you are in any contest, you should
work as if there were, up to the very
last minute, a chance to lose it.
This is battle, this is politics,
this is anything.
Dwight D. Eisenhower

Hard work is a legacy of generations
　　who settled the prairie, broke the soil,
　　built the sod houses, fought droughts
　　　　and grasshoppers.

Tom Brokaw

Industry.

Utah State Motto

Work conquers all things.

Oklahoma State Motto

Hard Work

It was a desolate, forgotten land, a stubborn, resisting land. Heroics wouldn't count for much here. It would take slow, backbreaking labor, and time, and the actions of the seasons to make the prairie bloom.

Edith Ammons Kohl

No moral man can have peace of mind if he leaves undone what he knows he should have done.

John Wayne

It's not what you pay a man, but what he costs you that counts.

Will Rogers

On the plains, luck, as well as hard work,
played an important role
in the settler's success.

Paula M. Nelson

You've got to be lucky, but then you've got
to be able to take advantage of your luck.

Chuck Conners

Words without actions are the assassins
of idealism.

Herbert Hoover

A good man is like a good horse. Turn his head loose and let him work.

"Kid" Marley

The days you work are the best days.

Georgia O'Keefe

Always take your job
seriously, but never
yourself.

Dwight D. Eisenhower

5

Adversity

Western pioneers were no strangers to adversity. Hardship was as much a part of the scenery as big mountains and buffalo herds. In 1847, Elizabeth Smith Geer wrote these words as she and her family inched toward the Oregon Territory: "It rains and snows. My children gave out with cold and fatigue. There was not one dry thread on one of us, not even my babe. I have not told you half we have suffered. I am not adequate to the task."

The Old West was more than a place, it was a test of endurance. Only the sturdiest and the luckiest survived. On the pages that follow, we hear from Westerners who learned about adversity the hard way. Thankfully, they were adequate to the task.

Adversity

We have learned to follow the customs
of the country, and get along as best we can
with what we have.

Mrs. Theodore Jorgenson

I shall never forget the utter loneliness
which almost overwhelmed me as we drove
under dark skies in the rain, over the prairies
with no path to follow. There was no human
habitation — only prairie and sky.

Fanny Malone

We were frightened and homesick.
Whatever we had pictured in our
imaginations, it bore no resemblance
to the tarpaper shack without comforts;
nor had we counted on the desolation
of prairie on which we were marooned.
This was not the West
I had dreamed of.

Edith Ammons Kohl

I've often been asked if we did not suffer with fear in those days, but I've said no we did not have enough sense to realize our danger.

Nancy Hembree Snow Bogart

This is home.
Here our children have been born — some
have died and lie buried in the soil
that has had no rain.

Clara Bentley Teter

It strikes me now that mothers on the road
had to undergo more trial and suffering
than anybody else.

Martha Ann Morrison

A man is not finished when he is defeated.
He is finished when he quits.

Richard M. Nixon

No one can defeat us unless we first
defeat ourselves.

Dwight D. Eisenhower

Failure? I think failure is quitting.

John Connally

Good people are good because
they've come to wisdom through failure.
William Saroyan

Tough times never last, but tough people do.
Robert Schuller

If we never had any storms,
we couldn't appreciate the sunshine.
Dale Evans

Pioneers or frontiersmen are a class of men
peculiar to our country and seem to have
been designed especially to meet
the exigencies of the occasion.

John C. Duval

The real empire builders will stay right here.
They will grapple with the difficulties
of pioneer life joyously.

E. L. Keith

Those who would survive the rigors
of this place must either be equipped to meet
the exactions imposed or to avoid them.

Dr. A. M. Woodbury

Our home was one of great plains, large
rivers, and wooded mountains. The winter
was cold. The winds were so strong they
made us feel their strength. The summers
were hot and violent. We grew used to
strength, height, distance, power.

Luther Standing Bear

Once I moved about like the wind.
Now, I surrender to you, and that is all.

Geronimo, 1886

Words are less needful to sorrow than joy.

Helen Hunt Jackson

Men suffering from hunger never talk much,
but rather bear their sorrows in moody
silence, which is much preferable
to fruitless complaints.

Jedediah Smith

When your hand is in the lion's mouth,
withdraw it quickly.

Sam Houston

When a man is finally boxed in,
and he has no choice, he begins
to decorate his box.

John Steinbeck

Remember Lot's wife. Never look back.

Richard M. Nixon

A dose of adversity is
often as needful as
a dose of medicine.

Pioneer Saying

With a dirt floor, you have fleas for sure.

Howard Ruede

The typical Nebraska homesteader
made his home of sod or dug a hole
in the side of a hill.

Cass G. Barns

Life is too short to live under a sod roof.

Native Nebraskan

We do not live, we only stay.
We are too poor to get away.

Old Pioneer Saying

Next year will be better
is the eternal hope
of those who suffer.

Clara Bentley Teter

Have faith.
It's contagious.

Sam Rayburn

6

Attitude

Walt Disney was born east of the Mississippi, but like countless Americans, he found his fortune in the West. In 1923 Disney arrived in a small California community called Hollywood. With a half-filled suitcase and a pocketful of dreams, Walt was on his way. Soon, his cartoons were winning Academy Awards, but more importantly, they were winning the hearts of movie fans everywhere.

In true Western fashion, Disney dared to think big. He once said, "If you can dream it, you can do it." But Walt was more than an idle dreamer; he backed up those dreams with creativity, hard work and perseverance.

Like Disney, the early pioneers left the security of the East for the promise of the West. Facing an uncertain future, these men and women managed to keep their spirits up. In the Wild West, hopes and dreams were as essential as horses and saddles.

History may debate many aspects of America's relentless march to the Pacific, but of one thing we can be certain: The West was won by optimists.

Confidence goes a long
way toward success.
And the confidence of
the Westerners is superb.

James Bryce

I'm happier because I made up my mind
to be that way.

Merle Haggard

Don't let what you cannot do interfere with
what you can do.

John Wooden

Trust in God and fear not.

Sam Houston

The secret of happiness is being yourself.

Dan Blocker

The tougher the fight, the more important the mental attitude.

Michael Landon

Don't believe in pessimism.

Clint Eastwood

If we find any peace or
happiness on this earth,
I suppose 99 percent of it
will be within our home.

Charley Wooster

A problem difficult at night is often
resolved in the morning after the
committee of sleep has worked on it.

John Steinbeck

P eople's minds are changed through
observation and not through argument.

Will Rogers

T o disagree, one doesn't have
to be disagreeable.

Barry Goldwater

Hope is desire and expectation
rolled into one.

Ambrose Bierce

We create our own unhappiness.
The purpose of suffering is to help us
understand we are the ones who cause it.

Willie Nelson

Too much self-pity will give you
a nervous breakdown.

Sid Richardson

If you think it's going to rain, it will.

Clint Eastwood

Right from the start, we are dying.
Live to the limit every minute of every day.
Whatever you want to do, do it now.

Michael Landon

Write of me not, "Died in bitter pains," but
"Emigrated to another star."

Helen Hunt

Again and again
the impossible problem
is solved when we see
that the problem is
only a tough decision
waiting to be made.

Robert Schuller

Cowboys were, as a rule,
very good natured.
In fact, it did not pay
to be anything else.

"Teddy Blue" Abbott

7

Pioneer Spirit

What drove the pioneers westward? They were driven by a strong need for independence and a burning desire for opportunity. Harry Lovald, Editor of the *Cheyenne Valley News* wrote, "The trouble with most of us is a restless spirit. Instead of making opportunity come to us, we are chasing our legs off running after it."

Whether searching for gold, buffalo hides, farmland or religious freedom, settlers of the Old West endured almost any hardship. Slowly, painfully, each pioneer family carved a living out of that wild new world. Here's to the spirit that made it all possible.

The American system is one of rugged individualism.

Herbert Hoover

Homesteading was the spirit of the times —
a big adventure.

Mary Bartels

The opportunity of doing exactly
as I pleased constituted for me one
of the chief charms of the prairie.

Ada Blayney Clark

What is there in the land-hunger that
inspires men to cross a continent and take
their place in a line for a chance in a hundred
to draw a quarter section? It is partly
the same spirit of adventure that sent
Jason searching for the Golden Fleece.

Yankton Press-Dakotan

Pioneer Spirit

If a man is disappointed in politics or love,
he goes and buys land. If he disgraces
himself, he betakes himself to a lot
in the West.

Harriet Martineau

On the open frontier, a person could
be reborn; he could have a second chance.

Harold Simonson

I began to feel much of my life would have
been wasted living in the outside world
imitating fashions, wondering about
neighbors' affairs, worrying about
my children's companions.

Kate Wenner

We were as much pleased with our fat
venison on the banks of the Salt Lake as
we would have been in the possession
of all the luxuries of a civilized life
in other circumstances.

Jedediah Smith

There is no "slippery slope" toward loss
of liberties, only a long staircase where each
step downward must first be tolerated by the
American people and their leaders.

Alan Simpson

Man is not free unless government
is limited.

Ronald Reagan

Our liberties we prize, and our rights
we will maintain.

Iowa State Motto

I am determined to cut every thread
and live free.

Brigham Young

Pioneer Spirit

It takes three log houses to make a city
in Kansas, but they begin calling it a city
as soon as they have staked out the lots.
Horace Greeley

America is a country of young men.
Ralph Waldo Emerson, 1844

There is a proud, undying thought in man
that bids his soul look upward
to fame's proud cliff!
Sam Houston

We were contented to let
things remain as the
Great Spirit made them.
The white men were not,
and would change the
rivers and mountains
if they did not suit them.

Chief Joseph

Pioneer Spirit

I never have seen so fine a population
as in Oregon. They were honest,
because there was nothing to steal;
sober, because there was no liquor;
there were no misers because there was
no money; they were industrious,
because it was work or starve.

Anonymous Pioneer

Where would you go? Back to the place
where you were dissatisfied with
before you came out here?

Davenport News

We are young and have life before us.
We cannot waste it here
in the Rocky Mountains.

Doc Newell, 1840

It's a corner of heaven itself,
  Though it's only a tumble-down nest,
With love brooding there, no place can compare
  With my little grey home in the West.

          Eardley Wilmot

Home, home on the range,
  Where the deer and the antelope play,
Where never is heard a discouraging word,
  And the skies are not cloudy all day.

      Anonymous Cowboy Song, circa 1860

The prospector is a man of imagination.
The spirit of unrest burns in his blood.

J. Ross Browne

Once started on the journey, the problem
was to finish. We didn't think much of the
unborn generations who would profit by
our venturesomeness. It was simply
a desperate undertaking.

Anonymous Pioneer

Above all things, the plainsmen had to have
an instinct for direction. I never had
a compass in my life, but I was never lost.

Charles Goodnight

The frontier is the line that separates
  the known from the unknown wherever
  it may be, and we have a driving need
    to see what lies beyond.

Louis L'Armour

Large quantities of moss stripped from
  the tree made a good mattress. With buffalo
robes and blankets we had comfortable beds.

Anonymous Settler

I would rather live as we do, in a sod house
we own, than to rent and have someone boss
    us around.

Nebraska Pioneer

Pioneer Spirit

Amid all the romance of the building of the
railroad we tend to forget that it was one of
the major industrial enterprises of its age.

T. H. Watkins

We who had grown accustomed to the sight
of the empty prairie, to whom the arrival of
the stage from Pierre was an event,
were overwhelmed by the confusion,
the avalanche of people moving steadily
across the trackless plains.

Edith Ammons Kohl

Once the rails were joined at Promontory,
I think you can say we began to think of
ourselves truly as a continental nation.

T. H. Watkins

Nothing would be the same in the West
after Promontory.

N. Scott Momaday

Homesteading would be so much harder
if it weren't for your good neighbors.

Edward Boyden

Never betray a friend or comrade
for the sake of your own gain.

Belle Starr

The horse thief was always the criminal
most hated and despised, and his punishment
was always summary and swift.

Emerson Hough

Equality before the law.

Nebraska State Motto

I'm going to Oregon, where there'll be
no slaves, and we'll all start even.

Johnny Minto

We must exchange the philosophy of excuse
for the philosophy of responsibility.

Barbara Jordan

All our lives we
are preparing to be
something or somebody,
even if we don't know it.

Katherine Anne Porter

It is a great responsibility
to be pioneers in
so great a world.

Narcissa Whitman

8

Big Nature

In 1813, an overly optimistic Robert Stuart wrote, "It appears that a journey across the continent of North America might be performed with a wagon, there being no obstruction in the wheel rout that any person would dare to call a mountain." In only a few years, Americans learned the gravity of Stuart's geographical miscalculation. Not only were the mountains much bigger than advertised, so were the deserts, the plains, and the canyons. The following quotations extol the virtues of Mother Nature's oversized progeny: the West.

We are in view of the ocean, this great Pacific Ocean which we have been so long anxious to see. Oh, the joy!

William Clark, 1805

Everything in the West is on a grander scale.

Edward Weston

Big Nature

The Rocky Mountains: grand forests,
grassy glades, frequent springs and dancing
streams. This place is destined to be
a favorite resort of civilized man.

Horace Greeley

Whoever wishes to see nature in all its
primitive glory and grandeur, in its almost
ferocious wildness, must visit the mountains
of Washington and Oregon.

Henry Custer

Rainier, from Puget Sound, is a sight
for the gods.

Paul Fountain

The distant mountain heights smoked
in the dawn like tired horses; the sun rose like
a disk of copper through the spindrift vine.

Alfred Lambourne

Yellowstone is one place where miracles
not only happen, but where they happen
all the time.

Thomas Wolfe

The Grand Canyon is carven deep by the
master hand; it is the gulf of silence,
widened in the desert; it is all time inscribing
the naked rock; it is the book of the earth.

Donald Culross Peattie

King Solomon in all his glory never had
a room in his palace that could compare with
the rooms of Carlsbad Caverns.

Robert Holley

The Mojave is a big desert and a frightening
one. It's as though nature tested a man for
endurance and constancy to prove whether
he was good enough to get to California.

John Steinbeck

Big Nature

The Badlands — they deserve this name.
A sense comes from it that it does not like or
welcome humans.

John Steinbeck

The Badlands look as you might expect
the moon to look if it were hot.

Douglas Reed

Between Amarillo and the North Pole,
there is nothing to stop the wind
but a barbed wire fence.

Pioneer Saying

Great Salt Lake, the Dead Sea of America.

Townsfolk of Corinne, Utah

The Wisdom of the West

The coyotes remind you that they are still
in possession of the plains at night.
Anonymous Homesteader

The tall grass heaves and plunges like
an ocean in its vast extent, in its monotony,
and in its danger.
Prairie Sportsman, 1850s

O wilderness of drifting sand,
O lonely caravan!
The desert heart is set apart,
Unknown to any man.
Walter Prescott Webb

The desert retaliates, it puts into operation
the natural law of self-defense.
Alfred Lambourne

Big Nature

Even against our will, the bigness and peace
of the open spaces were bound to soak in.
Edith Ammons Kohl

Masses of white clouds piled up against
the blue sky, shaped into giant torsos,
or thrones fit for the Gods.
John Hudson, 1850

The finest workers in stone are not copper
or steel tools, but the gentle touches of air
and water working at their leisure with
a liberal allowance of time.
Henry David Thoreau

Under certain conditions, a place becomes
part of us; we own it. We absorb it into our
lives. It cannot be taken from us. It is ours,
without title or deed.
Alfred Lambourne

See to it that ye pollute not your inheritance,
for if you do, you might expect that
the judgement of heaven will be poured
out upon you.
Anonymous Mormon Settler

Until you've walked on land that's never
been broken, and smell air that's never been
breathed, you don't know what clean is.
A Sooner's Daughter

If you don't get up and stir around
in the morning, you've missed
the best part of the day.
Watt Matthews

Every foot of what you call America
not very long ago belonged to the Red Man.
Chief Washakie

I never said the land was mine to do with
as I chose. The one who has the right
to dispose of it is the one who created it.
Chief Joseph

I love to roam over the prairies.
There I feel free and happy, but when we
settle down, we grow pale and die.
Satanta

The life of white men is slavery.
They are prisoners in towns or farms.
Sitting Bull

Everything on earth has a purpose,
every disease an herb to cure it, and
every person a mission. This is
the Indian theory of existence.
Mourning Dove

Nature makes the man to fit
his surroundings.
Luther Standing Bear

God is making the world, and the show
is so grand and beautiful and exciting that
I have never been able to study any other.

John Muir

Mountain parks and reservations are useful
not only as fountains of timber and irrigating
rivers, but as fountains of life.

John Muir

Let children walk with Nature.

John Muir

Climb the mountains and get their good
tidings. Nature's peace will flow into you
as sunshine flows into trees.

John Muir

The wilderness is
a necessity. Going
to the mountains
is going home.

John Muir

Give me men to match my mountains.

Inscribed on the California State Capitol

9

The States

In writing about America, Alistair Cooke once observed, "Nothing you say about the whole country is going to be true." The same could be said of the West. It is simply too big and too diverse for generalities. In this chapter, we consider a few relevant quotations about the states which comprise this rich diversity.

In Nebraska, the Middle West merges
with the West.

Federal Writers' Project

Kansas, in sum, is one of the finest states
and lives a sane, peaceful, and prosperous life.

Pearl Buck

Oklahoma is one of the friendliest states
in the union.

Ernie Pyle

Tejas

Indian word for friend

The province of Techas will be the richest
state of our Union without any exception.
Thomas Jefferson, 1820

Texas is the finest portion of the globe
that has ever blessed my vision.
Sam Houston

Dice 'em, boil 'em, mash 'em!
Idaho, Idaho, Idaho!

Idaho Football Cheer

I would never have been President if it had
not been for my experiences in North Dakota.

Theodore Roosevelt

South Dakota has been, and still is,
a pioneer state.

American Guide Series, 1938

The frantic bustle of America was not
in Montana. The calm of the mountains
and the rolling grasslands had got
into the inhabitants.

John Steinbeck

For a greatness of beauty I have never
   experienced anything like New Mexico.
                                    D. H. Lawrence

New Mexico has an austere and planetary
   look that daunts and challenges the soul.
                          Elizabeth Shepley Sergeant

Land of extremes. Land of contrasts.
   Land of surprises. Land of contradictions.
            That is Arizona.
                            Federal Writer's Project

The intangible element that makes Colorado
great is its climate.

American Guide Series, 1941

Colorado is going to be the playground
for the entire Republic. You will see this
as the real Switzerland of America.

Theodore Roosevelt, 1905

Utah's loveliness is a desert loveliness,
unyielding and frequently sterile.

Federal Writer's Project, 1941

Other people have
psychologists.
I have Utah.

Robert Redford

Nevada is one of the very youngest and
wildest of the states.

John Muir

The desolation of Nevada is awesome.

Neil Morgan

People on the Pacific Coast think
of themselves as belonging to the "coast";
the "West" is quite something else again.

John Gunther

Oregon is a large, rich, compact section
of the west side of the continent, containing
nearly a hundred thousand square miles of
deep, wet evergreen wood, fertile valley,
icy mountains, and high, rolling,
wind-swept plains.

John Muir

Few states are more fertile and productive
in one way or another than Washington.

John Muir

The green damp England of Oregon.

Alistair Cooke

California, more than any
other part of the union,
is a country by itself.

James Bryce, 1888

10

Native American Wisdom

When one hears the words "American settler," a certain mental image is evoked. One thinks of sailing ships, covered wagons, and log cabins. But the original American pioneers came on foot. Peter Iverson observed, "Perhaps thirty thousand years ago, the first settlers arrived in the land that would come to be known as North America. These pioneers did not travel by ship, nor did they claim any territory for any monarch, but they did discover America."

For countless generations, Native Americans lived in quiet harmony with their natural surroundings. Through their stories and legends, these spiritual people created societies founded upon respect for nature, respect for their neighbors, and respect for themselves. Sadly, these cultures have been nearly obliterated. Perhaps we need them more than ever.

With one smile, may there be enlightenment.

The Koshares' (Clown's) Prayer

We are here on this Earth to be teachers.
Terrance Honvantewa, Hopi Artist/Teacher

Act as if everybody were related to you.
Navajo Saying

Being Hopi is more a philosophy, an ideal.
Humbleness means peace, honesty — all
mean Hopi. We strive to be Hopi. Each person
must look into their heart and make changes
so that they may become Hopi when
they reach their destination.
Percy Lomaquahu

All men were made by the same Great
Spirit. They are all brothers. The earth is
the mother of all people, and all people
should have equal rights upon it.

Chief Joseph

Do you want wisdom? Go up on a hill
and talk to God.

Mathew King, Lakota Chief

The Great Spirit is in all things.
The Great Spirit is our father, but the earth
is our mother. She nourishes us.

Big Thunder

The Great Spirit knows no boundaries,
nor will his red children acknowledge any.

Tecumseh, Chief of the Shawnees

The Great Spirit sees and hears everything, and He never forgets.

Chief Joseph

Nobody on his own strength
        has ever succeeded.

Zuni Saying

Flexible strength is better than inflexible.
      Let the storm flow over you,
        and then pop back up.

Michael Kabotie, Hopi Artist

The essence of Pueblo life is acknowledging
    what you have and being thankful.

Diane Reyna, Santa Fe Video Producer

Whatever is happening in your life,
    that's where you get your peace from,
     and peace will give you patience.

Kalley Musial, Navajo Weaver

Man did not weave the web of life, he is merely a strand in it. Whatever he does to the web, he does to himself.

Chief Seattle

Native Americans are like Pima baskets:
the strongest part is the middle, the first part
to be made.

Earl Ray, Salt River Pima Indian

When we plant, we are showing our faith
in life.

Ramson Lomatewama

The Indian way is basically a spiritual way
of living. Being Indian is what you feel
in your heart.

Tony Ringlero, Apache/Pima

You are born with the spirit, but it's up
to you to be responsible to it, to develop
it in a way that you would be proud to say,
"I'm a Hopi," or "I'm a Navajo." It's a tradition.
It's a language. It's an identity.

Terrance Honvantewa, Hopi Artist/Teacher

The life of a man is a circle from childhood
to childhood, and so it is in everything
where power moves.

Black Elk

I came into this world to die. My body is
only to hold a spirit life. Should my blood be
sprinkled, I want no wounds from behind.
Death should come fronting me.

Toohoolhoolzote

There is no death, only a change of worlds.

Chief Seattle

Our fathers gave us many laws which they
had learned from their fathers. They told us
to treat all men as they treated us, that we
should never be the first to break a bargain,
that it was a disgrace to tell a lie, that
we should speak only the truth.

Chief Joseph

He who will steal an arrow
will steal a horse.

Native American Saying

Never criticize someone until you've walked
a mile in his moccasins.

Native American Saying

If a man loses anything and goes back and
looks carefully for it, he will find it.

Sitting Bull

Tell me, and I'll forget.
Show me, and I may not remember.
Involve me, and I'll understand.

Native American Saying

There are some animals you don't eat,
there are some animals you eat. Eat what the
birds eat. The birds, they know.

Hualapai Elder

These lands are ours. No one has a right
to remove us, because we were the first
owners. The Great Spirit above has appointed
this place for us, on which we light our fires,
and here we will remain.

Tecumseh, Chief of the Shawnees

So that they will respect the land,
tell your children that the earth is rich with
the lives of their kin. Teach your children
what we have taught our children,
that the earth is our mother.

Chief Seattle

A man who would not love his father's grave
is worse than a wild animal.

Chief Joseph

We depend on the Earth to make our living.
It's our social security.

John Lanza, Oraibi Elder

I have never taken a gift from the white man.
I never will. Their presents
make strong men soft.

Chief Joseph

Riches would do us no good. We could not
take them with us to the other world.
We do not want riches.
We want peace and love.

Red Cloud

When an Indian is shut up in one place,
his body becomes weak.

Sitting Bull

We have lived upon this land from days
beyond history's records, far past any living
memory, deep into the time of legend.
The story of my people and the story
of this place are one single story.
We are always joined together.

Taos Pueblo Indian

No one wants peace more than I.
I have killed ten white for every Indian's life
taken. But the white man is increasing,
while my tribe is growing smaller.

Cochise, Apache Chief

We were like deer.
They were like grizzly bears.

Chief Joseph

I am tired. My heart is sick and sad. From where the sun now stands, I will fight no more, forever.

Chief Joseph

It is painfully clear that the United States needs its Indians and their culture. It desperately needs the lessons of a culture that has a deep reverence for nature, and values the simple, the authentic, the humane.

Stewart L. Udall

11

The Wild West

Dee Brown wrote, "Americans know neither their country nor themselves unless they know the story of the old Wild West." Perhaps this explains our fascination with old-time cowboys. As we learn about them, we also learn about our history and ourselves.

Today, the West bears little resemblance to its wild, early days, but its mythology will not die. Western myth pits good against evil. It is a mythology of man against nature, of hope versus despair. The story of the Wild West is, in a sense, the story of humanity's individual and collective struggles.

American philosopher William Ernest Hocking wrote, "There are deeper myths, born of the permanent and universal aspirations of men. Such myths as these are never mere mythology, because they are founded on a literal and present truth."

No wonder the world loves a good Western.

Cowboy: The chief qualifications of
efficiency in this calling are courage
alertness, endurance, horsemanship,
and skill in the use of lariat.

Joseph Nimmo, Jr.

Though the cowboy's existence is hard and
dangerous, it has a wild attraction that
strongly draws to it his bold, free spirit.

Theodore Roosevelt

The cowboy is the predominant figure
in American mythology.

William W. Savage, Jr.

In characters, cowboys are like never was
or never will be again.

"Teddy Blue" Abbott

In the West, those who survived became a heroic race.

Frederic L. Paxson

It is an old saying on the plains:
A man without a horse has no business
on the prairie.

H. M. Stanley, 1895

Better to ride a poor horse then go afoot.

Cowboy Saying

A man without a horse is a man
without legs.

Cowboy Saying

The prettiest color of a horse is fat.

"Kid" Marley

A real cowboy always saddles
his own horse and kills his own snakes.
"Kid" Marley

A man or boy who can't ride in a new
country is about as valuable as a clerk
who cannot write in a city office.
Percy Ebbutt

There ain't a horse that can't be rode.
There ain't a man that can't be throwed.
Saying of the Old West

There was only two things the old-time
cowpunchers were afraid of: a decent woman
and being set afoot.
"Teddy Blue" Abbott

The Wild West

We cowboys were the salt of the earth,
   and we had the pride that went with it.
                        "Teddy Blue" Abbott

The West in the old days asked no questions
            of any man.
                        Emerson Hough

We take a man here and ask no questions.
   We know when he throws his saddle
   on a horse whether he understands
            his business or not.
                        Henry C. Hooker

Us cowboys wasn't respectable,
   but then again we didn't pretend to be.
                        "Teddy Blue" Abbott

The Texas Ranger rides like a Mexican,
trails like an Indian, shoots like a Tennessean,
and fights like a devil.

John S. Ford

Deringer pistols were designed
for effectiveness at short range —
across the poker table, for example.

William B. Edwards

Hospitality in the prairie country is not
limited. Even if your enemy passes your way,
you must feed him before you shoot him.

O. Henry

Come to Van Horn, Texas. The climate is
so healthy we had to shoot a man
to start our graveyard.

Placard, circa 1910

You never know your luck
till the wheel stops.

Western Saying

Give a man luck and sawdust will do
for brains.

"Kid" Marley

Ghost towns and dust bowls, like motels,
are Western inventions.

Wallace Stegner

Stockmen will have to yield to farmers.
They are to agriculture what the prospector
is to mining — merely the pioneers.

The Black Hills Journal, July 17, 1885

All my brothers were farmers except one, and he ended up the worst of the lot: a sheep man and a Republican.

"Teddy Blue" Abbott

Never allow a man to get
the drop on you.

Wild Bill Hickok

12

Observations on Dodge City, Vegas, Route 66 and Other Facts of Western Life

We conclude with a potpourri of Western wisdom. Enjoy.

Dodge City. Rowdiest town in Kansas.
Toughest town in the West.
Meanest place in the country.

Jim Hoy

Vegas is the most extreme and allegorical of
American settlements, bizarre and beautiful.

Joan Didion

Route 66 is the mother road.

John Steinbeck

It is very hard to give anything like an
   adequate conception of the size
      of the Grand Canyon.

John Muir

In the West, the past is very close.
   In many places, it still believes
      it's the present.

John Masters

We don't give our criminals
much punishment, but we sure give 'em
plenty of publicity.

Will Rogers

The less secure a man is, the more likely
he is to have extreme prejudice.

Clint Eastwood

There is nothing so skillful in its own defense
as imperious pride.

Helen Hunt Jackson

Any jackass can kick down a barn,
but it takes a good carpenter to build one.

Sam Rayburn

When I started counting
my blessings, my whole
life turned around.

Willie Nelson

Tomorrow comes to us at midnight very clean. It's perfect when it arrives, and it puts itself in our hands and hopes we've learnt something from yesterday.

John Wayne

About the time we make the ends meet,
somebody moves the ends.

Herbert Hoover

You are born and can't help it,
and you'll die the same way.

"Kid" Marley

The Indians have long opposed all efforts
of white men to enter the Black Hills, but I
have a well-equipped force, strong enough
to take care of itself.

George Armstrong Custer

The only sure thing about luck is that
it will change.

Bret Harte

For every nation and every individual,
    the principal worry is debt.

Will Rogers

If you want to know how a man stands,
    go among the people who are
      in his same business.

Will Rogers

A fanatic is always the fellow
    on the opposite side.

Will Rogers

The more ignorant you are,
    the quicker you fight.

Will Rogers

One way to solve the traffic problem would be to keep all the cars that aren't paid for off the streets.

Will Rogers

Nothing makes a man as mad as the truth.

Will Rogers

Politics has gotten so expensive that it even takes a lot of money to get beat.

Will Rogers

History doesn't repeat itself, but it rhymes.

Mark Twain

Even if you're on the right track, you'll get run over if you sit there long enough.

Will Rogers

It's great to be great
but it's greater
to be human.

Will Rogers

Sources

Sources

John Louis O'Sullivan 18
Frederic L. Paxson 137
Donald Culross Peattie 99
Katherine Anne Porter 28, 41, 42, 93
Ernie Pyle 110
Earl Ray 126
Sam Rayburn 35, 68, 148
Ronald Reagan 83
Red Cloud 131
Robert Redford 115
Douglas Reed 100
Diane Reyna 124
Albert Deane Richardson 23
Sid Richardson 33, 75
Tony Ringlero 126
Francois De La Rochefoucauld 37
Will Rogers 28, 30, 31, 34, 36, 47, 52, 74, 148,
    152, 153, 154
Theodore Roosevelt 45, 46, 112, 136
Darrell Royal 50
Howard Ruede 66
William Saroyan 28, 61
Satanta 104
William W. Savage, Jr. 136
Robert Schuller 61, 77
Chief Seattle 125, 127, 130

WG

About the Author

Criswell Freeman is a Doctor of Clinical Psychology living in Nashville, Tennessee. He is the author of *When Life Throws You a Curveball, Hit It* and *The Wisdom Series* from WALNUT GROVE PRESS. He is also a published and recorded country music songwriter.

About Wisdom Books

Wisdom Books chronicle memorable quotations in an easy-to-read style. Written by Criswell Freeman, this series provides inspiring, thoughtful and humorous messages from entertainers, athletes, scientists, politicians, clerics, writers and renegades. Each title focuses on a particular region or special interest.

Combining his passion for quotations with extensive training in psychology, Dr. Freeman revisits timeless themes such as perseverance, courage, love, forgiveness and faith.

"Quotations help us remember the simple yet profound truths that give life perspective and meaning," notes Freeman. "When it comes to life's most important lessons, we can all use gentle reminders."

The Wisdom Series

by Dr. Criswell Freeman

Regional Titles

Wisdom Made In America	ISBN 1-887655-07-7
The Book of Southern Wisdom	ISBN 0-9640955-3-X
The Wisdom of the Midwest	ISBN 1-887655-17-4
The Wisdom of the West	ISBN 1-887655-31-X
The Book of Texas Wisdom	ISBN 0-9640955-8-0
The Book of Florida Wisdom	ISBN 0-9640955-9-9
The Book of California Wisdom	ISBN 1-887655-14-X
The Book of New York Wisdom	ISBN 1-887655-16-6
The Book of New England Wisdom	ISBN 1-887655-15-8

Sports Titles

The Golfer's Book of Wisdom	ISBN 0-9640955-6-4
The Wisdom of Southern Football	ISBN 0-9640955-7-2
The Book of Stock Car Wisdom	ISBN 1-887655-12-3
The Wisdom of Old-Time Baseball	ISBN 1-887655-08-5
The Book of Football Wisdom	ISBN 1-887655-18-2
The Book of Basketball Wisdom	ISBN 1-887655-32-8
The Fisherman's Guide to Life	ISBN 1-887655-30-1

Special Interest Titles

The Book of Country Music Wisdom	ISBN 0-9640955-1-3
The Wisdom of Old-Time Television	ISBN 1-887655-64-6